The Found Poet

summer

a collection of poetry by

TIM 2 TAYLOR

TAYLOR PRODUCTIONS

JACKSONVILLE

The Found Poet™is a trademark of Tim Taylor Productions, Inc.

The Found Poet - summer
First Printed Edition - 2013
First Digital Edition - 2013

Published by Tim Taylor Productions, Inc.
7536 Pottsburg Landing Drive
Jacksonville, Florida 32216

www.thefoundpoet.com
tim2taylor@facebook.com
#tim2taylor

Written by Tim 2 Taylor
Designed by Tim 2 Taylor
Edited by Tim 2 Taylor
Cover base image: iStockPhoto

Library of Congress Control Number -

Taylor, Timothy, 1960 -

Manufactured in the United States
ISBN - 978-0-9833382-0-8 (book)
ISBN - 978-0-9833382-2-2 (e-book)

Printed copys by
Lightning Source Inc.
14 Ingram Blvd.
La Vergne, TN USA 37086
1. Poetry
Distributed by Tim Taylor Productions, Inc.
To purchase copies in bulk please contact: (904)-238-0889

To book Tim 2 Taylor for personal appearances, book signings or motivational
speaking engagements, please call (904) 238-0889 or contact Tim 2 through
the website at www.thefoundpoet.com

Be sure to read the companion to this book *The Found Poet- winter*
Look for my weight-loss and fitness book *Fat As My Dad*
Watch for my two new books "Power 2 Stretch™" and "Life Loops™"

Life is made up of small comings and goings.
And for everything we take with us,
there is something that we leave behind.
            - Herman Raucher
            - from the book "Summer of 42"

CONTENTS

PREFACE

I never expected this. One day on a busy street corner I caught the cry of a brave voice shouting to be heard. The rambling aggressive sound of pure youth. A door to door poet selling his wares to anyone who cared to listen. I did.

From a child I've been an artist of some sort, drawing, painting, designing always creating something. Around the same age as the street poet 15 maybe 16 tops, I discovered my love of words as sculpting clay.

At that age everything pours freely from you. So it was with me and words. But time and grime of a hurried life turned the faucet of my words down to a trickle and eventually to a barren desert.

I had no found bravery. No white sail to set into the worldly winds. A quiet voice lived, yet never heard. So my words became as vanishing smoke.

But on this day, amongst the hustled city din, I borrowed some bravery from the youthful poet. I felt the wild wind and knew in that full sail instant I wanted my voice to be heard. For the first time I read aloud a poem I'd written for everyone to hear. (See: *Living through the sixties page 33*) This was the birth of me "The Found Poet."

So at the ripe age of 52, and having found my youthful bravery, I've decided to set my words free here in my first collection of poems. I hope you can discover something universal in my words, even if it's just a smile. These words have been my sanctuary, my recovery, my restitution, my kept joy and my long salvation.

I pray that it encourages you to borrow some bravery and raise your sails catching some of the wild wind within your own life.

Tim 2 Taylor

I breathed in church

I determined
my need
to walk a while
and find solace
in the silence
of trees

And enter into the
timbered sanctuary
of God's very nature

In a real attempt
to quiet the
worldly thoughts
that run amok
dangling thinly
in my life

in the still moment
I recognize
the chipper voices
of the small creatures
that I hurriedly ignore daily

mystically now transformed
into the ever present
choirs of freely
offered up praise

the very sound
of this translucent
blue day
compels me to kneel
in efforts to get closer
to the living deep deity

I appreciate the effortlessly
simple complexity
of the bee's colorful
resting spot

The tremendously treacherous,
random mountainous path
the truly committed
red ant has taken

And find myself moved
by the sheer multitudes
of tiny lives
lived amongst
the blades green

I catch a glimpse of
the harmonious dancing
to and fro
of the cardinal
and his singing wife
building their feathered lives
in the y of the swaying oak

then to gaze so closely
at the aging veins
of the now rusty
amber resting leaf
that told me his old man
glory days tale
of living in the wild wind
from birth

My quiet redemption
so loudly found
drops free from my eyes
the uncomplicated intimacy fills me
with warm heart's fire

I breathed in church
and uttered my own
prayer of praise
up aloud

And remember
graciously
the forgotten face
of my Savior
and we laughed freely
together

Blacksmith

In the darkness
a door is opened
Orange illuminates
a face
the blacksmith me

my ore
of raw emotions
faces the flames
once more
for I want iron
strong black metal

Rage red
warm flaming orange
ever yielding yellow
finally holy white
melts my thoughts
into the workability
of words

Radiant heat that overwhelms
emerge from the cleansing flame
from the stoked roar
to take your place
on lifes' anvil

Draw me over
pull taut the edges
lay me out

that I may come
before the forging place

Mighty arm swing
fall oh hammer
against the anvil of my heart
strike you strong
while the iron is hot

Beat upon my chest
rain down repeatedly
as my ribs tremble
at the thunder clap
clang

Take shape o malleable words
sculpt new or old
but take form
pleasurably

For I will quench you
and baptize you whole
on white linen
strong black metal
words

Hawk point

For many a year
they've come with spring
for me to gleefully watch
their daily routine

a splendid male hawk
and his calmly feathered wife
perched way atop
the sprouting lofty scrub oak

he always sits a branch
higher than her
maybe he's a chauvinist
I'm not sure

I choose to believe
it's a gentle arrangement
they've worked out
like an old married couple

for he spies and cries
she flees and flies
swoops and drops
downward upon

pray of the simple slow squirrel
or the cornered confused rabbit
maybe a minutive moving mouse
even the slithering speedy snake

Regardless
regale on tree top branch
he calls again his undying love
always she distantly replies

Lunch is ready
and away he flies

The rain has a name

Under an African sky
the Massi warrior stands
observing the savanna that
stretches out before him

long scorched
by the radiant orb overhead
the Kenyan dust
swirls up
behind each footstep

suddenly a familiar wind blows upon his skin
and its aroma carries a remembrance
that he longs for from his childhood

first a drop, then another
a sudden downpour

rain

he whispers the words... "a mvua ina a jina "
translation..."the rain has a name"

the proud warrior looks to the sky
with open raised arms
as if welcoming a lost lover
back into his loving embrace

he speaks it's name into the air... "ema nenos"
translation... "kind words"

the drops splash upon his hot face
and into his open mouth

"ema nenos anguko juu angu kavu moyo"
translation... "kind words fall upon my dry heart"

fufua mie
translation... "renew me"

He grins and wipes the water from his eyes
and continues on his journey homeward.

For A Season

I find myself this morning
lost in the verse of Neruda
and his amazing way
of lashing together
woman, and wonder and wild
to nature and tethered heart

His words move me
to think of the dormant
tulip and lilies bulbs
secured in a box
there in my garage

And how soon
on a crisp spring day
I shall retrieve them
from the dusty shelf
and I will give them back
to the earth
from whence they came

I'll plant them
like a prayer
of kneeling asking hope
not for God's immediate reward
nor golden answer now

But to wait
for a season
to understand that
my lifted voice is heard
and the toll of my hands
is for a reason

For at the first thaw of spring
the amber warm face of the jonquil
will smile wryly in my life
and the crimson tulips
shall wave good morning to me
from their beds
the lilies shall beckon me
to the clear blue sky

And the new life of spring
sweet prayers answered
repeatedly
glorious colorful truths
for others to see
and I will reside with them
once again
for another spring of me.

Short Smiling Monk

They spun like orange leaves in the wind
draped in rich crimson

their foreign words spoken
softly to an another's heart

the earth's very sounding bell
caught rays of morning

a short long distance call
I'm without a real understanding

still their tone
resonates pure in the air

in the thick wooden beams
and within my bone cold core

truth

the short smiling monk
brings me to exuberant sitting

to be in a place
of open enchanting prayer song

my face finds the warmth
and smiles universally

and I decide offer
a prayer up

with him
this day

Joy simple

Like the dangling feet
of my child
toes skyward
sailing on a swing

flying laughter at belly's drop
higher, push me higher
gentle innocent smile
exposes the grand experience

of earlier days
on sunny afternoons
spent in the air
free swinging

the salient sensation
of being off the ground
and being little
in a world so big

the clutching chest breath
of simply letting go
knowing the flowing
of moving to and fro

the first thing I built my daughter
was a swing
for I wanted to show her
joy simple

to always be able to find it
there in a seat
supported by chain
a way to fly

it's my heart held photograph
a snapshot of a gift
the wonderful memory
of her swinging joyous

a certain freshness

The pillows smelled of sunshine,
an aroma children today don't know
as their linens are dried
in mechanical tumbling machines
a modern convenience deprived

never having seen
clothes on a line
damp white linen of surrender
in the back yard
flagging in the summer breeze

who's moisture wick
by the sun for the price
of the fragrance
a transaction left behind

she laid her head down
and I beside her
on the newly made bed
we breathed in

sunshine soaked cotton
a certain freshness
in each others lives

butterfly

the butterfly landed upon my arm
and began whispering a poem

of little spry words
of God's ear
and first romance

of innocent laughter
of warm earnest conversations
and the mystery of those who dance

of a heart's stirrings
of a morning's rooster distant crow
and of the moons' personal phases

of last Wensday afternoon
of old songs on the radio
and a child's box of colorful crayons

of missed kisses
of autumn's cool breezes
and suddenly she flew away

such is life

Old friends

The lilies have poked there heads
up from under their soil covers
after a fortnight of slumber

The aspiring larks spring song
has awoken them this brilliant morning
It's alleluia to see them again
for the Gospel comes after the singing
and I've missed the color
of my old friends in my life

Whose sharp emerald blades small
herald their arrival to my door
and new friends
shall come to visit too

The invisible winged
blue breasted hummingbird
Several dexterous crawling Chameleons
and the fuzzy floating
white faced bumblebees

All playing like joyous children
free handed in my backyard
I'm ready after this winter's cold
to welcome them all to my home

Mother, may I go out and play too?

The student

Master, tell me of light?

Laughing,
sit and learn child.

When the candle gives it's light
does it not burn?

There cannot be light without the fire.

So when you feel life's burning
are you not giving off light?

Are we not stardust?

Behold the constellations
they have burned all of their fuel
millions of years ago.

Yet we still see their light.

So Master, what is
the nature of light?

Its nature is in the burning.

Living through the sixties

When men
used fire hoses
spraying hatred
tried to put out
another mans fire

Jesus hanging on the crucifix

When children
carried signs
with words
tyring to say
what was in there hearts
for others to see

Women burned their bras

When bombs
dropped from the sky
exploding people
I never got the chance
to actually meet

Men had casual sex

When television
shook with Elvis
and screamed with the Beatles
we watched raw talent
in black and white

A boy held the balloon by a string

When husbands
drank and smoked
and wives took pills
and were blind mutes
raising generation gapped
wide eyed optimist

Disney was in color

When music
discovered it had a voice
a needle in a groove
that could shape
a profit picture
AM went to FM
and we bought the 45s

The DJ took our request

When leaders
took bullets
in their heads
before they learned
to take the lives
of the people
they claimed to lead

Jon-Jon saluted the casket

When peace
with all it's signs
necklaces
strung around our necks
had a chance
in a bed
with John and Yoko

And even that truth was murdered

When years
pass as they all do
just one thing changed
one thing forever
ourselves

And the ball dropped in Times Square

It's 1970

*Inspired, I first performed this live on a street corner
in San Francisco. It was the first time I let my poet
voice be heard. It will never be the last.*

The Found Poet

A street poet yelling his words
proudly to the tourist who snap-shot
his snippets of zealot words
never slowing a second to listen

But I did

I smiled widly at his angry thoughts
as he was far too young
to have all the pull of gravity
he was hoping to emote

Yet I loved his verve

Pure youthful exuberance
his joyous fearless heart beating
a fire that burned so brightly
it touched fire to me

In a moments spark

I introduced myself
to ask if I could share a poem with him
so eagerly he opened his ears
as only another poet could

A child's first words

starting silent and low
my voice found I just let it go
for a minute they drew near
actually stopping to hear

Me... the found poet

reacting with hoots and hollers
and went off with smiles
shook my hand and thanked me
for simply sharing words

Born powerfully alive

the long dark me
danced under the sun
like a child free
in a wild crossing feild

Finally heard

and what I observed
in the eyes of the young black man
and the woman who sat upon the bench
and the walking Hispanic man
and the waiting others

was acceptance

To be so brave

Tell me oh youth
what pulls you
to be so brave

to venture out
onto soft soil
and plow the furrow

laying the seeds
of hope there
to harvest a new dream

I so love the fierceness
and the full leaping
of the young

oh that I might
firefly capture
the smallest light of it

in my days of age
to be a brave man
once more

It's own tail

Laughing out loud at the sight,
as the puppy chases it's own tail.
Round and around
growling and snapping
this direction and that.
"Daddy, doesn't he know that
he can't catch his own tail?"
He smiled
saying he knew a lot of people
who do the same crazy thing.
"Will he ever stop?" she asked.
"Soon he'll tire himself out
and move on to chasing the cat,
who's chasing after a bird,
who's chasing after a worm,
who's chasing after the dirt.
It seems we are all chasing
something
we just can't seem to catch
But it sure is fun to watch
isn't it?"

Watermelon

Some days I feel
like a watermelon
accidentally dropped
on a summer sidewalk
all burst open
cracked wide
innards splayed out
running red
full of seeds and thought
meat and rind
too full
too heavy
ripe ruby to hold
Oh well...
no use crying over
busted melon
Anyone got salt?

I came to touch a tree

I walked till I found her
rising grandly after all
these wondering years

as a boy I'd touched her bark
sable skinned cracked
evergreen ripe aroma of pine

her arms had beckoned
to climb and know her life
swiftly to the top highly

with God's downward gaze
seen for the first time
I felt her standing aliveness

a tree so grand
and felt the presents of an angle
floating there just above her

upon whos constant urging
she did ever grow
skyward

to find myself
after all these seasons
I came to touch a tree

realizing it was she
who in truth
had touched me

This boy who came to climb me

He touched my sable skin
dared to pull me in his clutches
up, upward climbing

standing gangly upon my arms
moving to the heights
of my evergreen tower

I've seen him daily
playing lowly beneath me
So why climb me now?

Why does he come
to hold me so closely
as if his life depended on it?

I can't understand why
the hours and days he's spent
within my branches

Oh to know his fantastic thoughts
as he looks outward
this boy who came to climb me

Maybe it's something I have
my wooden ringed heart
or my tall standing strength?

I pray o angle protect this boy
keep him safe here in glories wind
bring him pure back to ground

The Cellist

Play your cello
so deeply
fingers on my soul
bow across my heart

the articulation
timbre of aged willow
that pushes me to passions
vibrato with sweet attitude
that pulls fresh air into my lungs

moving stone walls
like tidal waves crash
you move me
move me
move
forward on a journey

to a note
written long ago
yet so new to my ears
like holding a first lover
curvy and warm
in the night

I yearn for more
of your melody
within me.

Passion

Passion is the first guest
to leave the party
so I could never paint
with color the red
as it no longer flowed
in my veins

a childhood life of flatness
blues and grays
a blacken days page
bludgeoned worthless works
on odd shaped canvas

sstrange
that with tears
and a whispered voice
that I would find red again

Red in your lipstick
Red in autumn leaves
surprisingly Red hair
Red in tangent words
Red in your touch

Red, red, red again

My agony a billion times
removed by your Red
The simple Red trill that resonates
though life itself
the spectrum begins with Red

love if Red
were the only color
your brought to me
the worlds' wealth pale

for in its mixture
Red gives sunrise
royal deep purple nights
Red hues of amber glow
fire strokes of heat unquenchable

In mornings I walk briskly
across the flourishing field
down a dirt road
nowhere near sunset
to raise my easel and paint anew
fresh cherry Red
with every bristle full

Because
you knocked
at my front door
and I let you in
my new love
Passion

love love

whistle whistle little bird
singing to the morning

babble babble gentle brook
tell the story of your long journey

buzz buzz fuzzy bee
show me the results of your shopping

flutter flutter lemon butterfly
brightly into the bluest of skies

croak croak spotted toad
hop to your shaded resting place

swim swim silver fish
leaping for your elusive lunch

love love

My bright yellow kite

The gust caught my hair
and stirred my mind
of a day long ago
which made me smile decidedly

to open the closet
and rummage through
life's accumulations
of assorted odds and ends

I know it's here
somewhere
tucked behind
and out of sight

Here it is
old friend
my bright yellow kite
of Chinese decent

untangle the twine
and fold out it's wings
too many years
in the darkness of my closet

Out to the sun
and his friend the wind
open space
and breath
I raise you up

catch your love
running headlong
without cold fear or rampant regret

Aloft you soar
unwind and drift
squint into the blueness
regal amber bird

The constant tug
pulls from within me
to the lost child
hiding in that closet

I smile
for I'm where my
golden soul
should be

In the taken indigo sky
full of sail
above it all
flying
my bright yellow kite.

Near the roots

Home the countryside
of my Italian past
low stone walls built with hands
the kicked up redden clay swirls
over the ivy covered trellis tell of my youth

memories like cooking pigs
childishly play with me
along with photographs framed
on lace laden tables
and plaster chips just there upon the floor

the air of ripe vines
fields away roll
my sky long sunset dreams
God's finger painted canvas
displayed in my own museum

the waters' patter
from the spitting fount
ever refreshing summered lips
like the curves of her
upon my bed

time saunters slowly
under the mighty shade tree
away from the boil of the Tuscan sun
my words lay near the roots
reach for the heart of my soil

I remember the day
of leaving her
to sail for this distant land
her eyes never to see again
an endless deep well

still she comes with me
in my bags of travel
backcountry grass
warm under my bare feet

how can I not
taste still the wine
and see the line of her earth

Summer sheets

White linen
freshly washed
hung on a line
on a summers day

A gentle wind flutters
as the suns' warmth
evaporates away
the abiding dampness

Leaving in its place
trapped so tightly
in the cotton weave
the suns very essences

Once unfurled upon a bed
reveals all it's mysteries

The white soft touch
that familiar smell
the enveloping comfort
it's inherent warmth

the restfulness of breathing in
summer sheets with you

Silk road

You have looked into my blue,
could you ever except the birds in my sky?

Turn the cup and drink from my tea?

Would you ever fold your hands and gather water
to pour upon my dry skin?

Your breasts like ice covered peaks
allow the sherpa in me to explore?

Loosen the silk robe and allow
me to embrace your oriental body?

Would you love me like a broken winged sparrow
and cry tenderly upon my feathers?

Kneel next to my wounded body
and except the birds in my sky?

Could you learn my inscrutable and exotic customs
and walk with me on this silk road?

The mountain which has called me

The mountain has called me
to tread always upward
under the ever-present flags
which color the wind

walking into the smiling
of those who embrace happiness
like no other I've found
causes my cracked lips to smile a return

my face blistered by the bluest sky
hides the burning felt in my lungs
taking one more gentle step
toward the mind of enlightenment

their kindness
has become my Tenzing
their tea warms me true
my load lightened by humble laughter

Tengboche climatizes me
the bells and forest
I spin Om Mani Padme Hum
like all the others on this rotating orb

I have not come to conquer
nor to flag a peak
a distant traveler
I have only come to seek

The mountain which has called me

White desert

I met her at the base
of the Great Pyramid
loping along with other tourist
both seemed out of place

her smile brilliantly stood
against the blue of noon
like a childhood crush
we look upon the old
feeling the new

we first spoke at a small table
of an outdoor cafe
and made up our minds
to leave the group
and explore the white desert

whistling golden winds
took us gazing
upward, outward, inward
for the first time
in ages
richly

on our own
she was on a stage of life
overlooked by those of youth
she herself possibility forgotten
the beauty possessed of her tender days

eye lines that had lived
still softer than one might imagine
noticing the sheerness of her blouse
as the wobbling wails
of a dedicated praying man
lifted off in the distance

the forgotten taste
of a unexpected kiss
stumbled upon together
sitting silent
yet saying so many things
over warm herb tea

always destined for distance
she removed her shoes
and decided to touch my heart
unearthing ancient relics found in foreign lands
a sunset seen as no other

she had to rejoin her group
leaving me alone in life's empty lobby
breathing differently than ever before
I'm soulfully happy
and the pyramids still stand

Roll upon me sweetly

Wash upon this sandy heart
tide does return
from whence it came

Leaving an amber shell
where nautical creatures
once slept

Ocean's roar
waves upon my chest
shaking me to my feet

Mighty lifting
buoyant once more
roll upon me sweetly
sweep me out
to your blueness

What tales of the briny deep
lie beneath your tropical waters
what shore come you
what treasures below
what surfaces
again and again

Salty skin to my lips
on this slight day.

Make me a lunch

I will come to you at noon
make me a lunch
of delightful fruit
and newborn bread

Pour vintage wine
into my glass
feed my soul
and nourish my body

For I've broken the earth
and labored seeding
before I return to furrow
beneath an afternoon of sun

Give me a lunch
among thy cool grass
spread for me
strawberry and honey

Renew my vigor
restore the breath in my chest
and I will return to you
upon days end

with wild meat and game
roots and leafs
to boil over thy fire
and dine with you

under the heavenly stars
until your fullness
faints you into sleep
in my arms

Will you make me a lunch?

Boat builder

I can reason now
as sands have fallen
and I've taken shape
under your hands

my woodworker
dragging your sharpen plain
across my rough timber
knots into dust

casting your eye
across my bow
stroking your hand
across my finished skin

boat builder
build me stoutly
destine me
for sail
under the endless sky

for travel far I will
distant and new
others will I ferry
cargo and treasures
hold and carry

for you have shaped me
to sail your waters
maker o maker
my ship of dreams

analog heartbeat

your love so analog
like a needle on record
dropped onto a groove
our music just plays

spiraling inward
in linear progression
of the original artist's recording
sweet sixties reverberations

lyrics from a distant dime dropped
freshly alive in my ears
a rhythm that can't be found
easily anymore

crassly digitally sampled
and computer produced now
but not with you
my long playing love

how I enjoy listening
soft in arms dancing
to the analog heartbeat
of you

Articulate interpellation

The only difference
between
us and them
is the blessing
and the curse of
articulate interpellation

They rail against us
and call us names
like heretic
for the words
we write

or eccentric
for the canvass
we paint

or starving artist
for pursuing
the music we play

or madly esoteric
for the images
we capture
and the stories
we act out
on film or stage

and yet

they read us
after we are dead
our body buried
or consumed with flame

they pay good money
to stand in silent grand rooms
to look upon our masterpieces

they feed their souls
on our songs
they sing from the heart

they escape their
morbid normalcy
seated in the dark
crying over the
love story on the screen

They always
in the fin
call us an impresario
a visionary,
genius or talented

Follow your artist heart
for the thems
will never understand
you

Unheard

Watch the people
scurrying to and fro
a day among the gray
squares they call life

and their you were
brown feathered bird
gazing downward from
your heavenly perch

you had to speak
high and clear
full of youthful vibrancy
declaring the beauty of this day

not like a warning
more like a holy song of praise
that would shame songs
found in vaulted cathedrals

they never heard you
scurrying ants
rushing to obscurity
gathering there pittances

a rich fortune
laid before them
given freely rarely touched
from an unheard bird

I heard you

Crayola cravings

I try my best to stay within the lines
of the coloring book
you've opened for me

But you've given me
a new box of 64 Crayolas
with a sharpener built right in the box!

I want so badly
to use every color
on your picture

Inside the lines
one color at a time
just won't do with you

Persimmon Cream, and Jade Fire
Purple Passion and Golden Apple
Flamingo Pink and Lemon Twist

Beautiful colores du jour

I want to mix the colors
with free-form strokes
to color your world

Just like the way
you've brought brilliant colors
back to my page.

fire flies in a jar

Glimmering in the night
elusive child's dance
the chase
hands together
to catch the prize

wiggles of small life
held glowing
carefully placed
in a jar
not enough

so off for more
frolicking in the dark
grabbing at the ambiguous
blackness

clasping what little treasures
you can find
screw down the lid
to place on your night stand
and illuminate your sleep

only to awaken
to find a little more death
at the bottom of your jar

out into the day
you shake the remains
and the few survivors
on to the grass
for you dad to mow over

From the dryer

Your arms
when they are
around me
feels like
clean warm towels
fresh from the dryer
on a rainy afternoon.

Handwritten

Retrieving the letter
from the mailbox
seeing it written
by her hand
made the distinction

clearly wrote
in a predestined way
the forceful curl
and the subtle slant
cursively

the tempo
embolden strokes
a fervency apparent
torrents
the words pour
down on paper
so eloquently
still
like a watercolor

nonetheless with a
directed conciseness
that only a woman
deep in the throws
of heartache
trying hard
to stand up again
can compose
within acquiesces

the spattered words
of her bare soul
broken open
like a pomegranate
seedy blood soaked fruit
spelling out her wishes

summarizing
certain anguish
alone
not a breath of disdain
but of gentle gratitude
for what had been given
and what remains
amongst the rubble
she finds herself
standing in yet again

a letter that ends
with the words
*"The sensation of your hugs
shall never leave me."*
a handwritten goodbye
without hope of
eternal redemption
my heart left me

- A poem I wrote 27 years ago

Fairly

downcast forgotten
harshly disregarded
flagrant invisibility
the anguish of others

mistreatment
so long taut
stretched to the point
of ripping in two
a soul crying darkness

how resplendent
when without a second
of thought or consequence
to be treated fairly
by a kind heart
in the daylight

it sparks a fire
that is not easily
ever extinguished
on this earth

this I've found to be truth

Dreamer of dreams

Like a young girls
mornings pickings

pressed between
pages of a romantic poets words

tucked secretly
in a hard bound book

left to slowly dry
preserved

as a remembrance
of the day of choice

I too feel
like a flower of your past

held and breathed in
orignal colorful glory

ripe and blue
unfolded wax paper protection

hold me in your hands
once more

allow time to slip
impossibly backwards

and feel
the heart of youth

true love as new again
shining so in your eyes

sweet dreamer of dreams

I'm flying

I land on this bridge daily
the one your tender hands
built for me

and resting upon its crest
I gaze long at the constant flow
running beneath me

I fold downward into the waters
cupping the cool sweet memories
only to drink of you once more

the aroma of the trees
catches me aware today
and to their call I listen

to the air I take
breathing strongly inward
my breast heaving full

I'm flying
only to realize I live in the halo
which you have left me

I often feel the place
where you reset
my broke wing

still to this day it holds me
heavenward under the sun
among the silver-edged billows

oh angle woman
to have known the warmth
of your hearts fire

it shall be
my winged soul
forever

within this blue day
as seen through your eyes
every beating feather

loves anew
the sky you've painted
that I find myself aloft in

Ode to marigolds

More orange than the sun
tiny flower
of children's song
bloom your abundance
on this last day
of March sunny

hang around the necks
of gurus and holy men
and let your sharp
fragrance move free
In the warming morning air

how from a boy
I have loved
the hue of you
drawn I have been
as sure as the small bee
seeks you out
so to I

a poor man planter
yearly the seed of you
I hide like gold
under earth
only to await
your smiling amber face
always turning skyward

pray I wrap myself
in your scalloped edges
orange
and reawaken the holy man
lost in the winters white
renew my soul
sweet Marigold fire

au sein Clair de lune

In the movement of three
to trip the light fantastic
like bare toes in low grass
and rain that falls softly on a pond
deep in the forest green

tears of love shed by a young girl
her heart that illuminates
like that of simple moonlight
cascading with opalescent candor
over keys to moving my musical heart

resonate oh chords of love
float here so far above me
yet be my ready earth
dip thy hand into my waters
and bring to your lips l'eau fraîche (*cool water*)

like a child's dance pure
spinning boldly in the pale
canopy of stars
to rapture me quietly
into this rarest of nights

the moon itself
watches over us fully
softly laughing
at the love found
au sein Clair de lune (*within moonlight*)

Electrically charged summer rain

The wind
whipped the clothes
sideways on my clothesline

fiercely flapping
like grand flags
proudly displayed
on the fourth of July

It's tattering tell
forecast of the approaching
summer storm

hurriedly plucking
the ripe crisp clothes
before the first quarter
sized drops fall
solemnly upon my head

running barefoot back
to the overhanging shelter
of my own porch

just before the crackle
of thunder precedes
the bottom dropping out

and the sweet arrival
the unmistakable smell of
electrically charged summer rain
reaches my nose

I have to laugh out loud
at the Lord's
delightful dancing drops
bouncing and playing
freely running wild

like excited children
at a birthday party
after too much cake

I take a seat
in my weathered wooden chair
just to take a look
and listen
to the speaking earth

I silently pray
asking for forgiveness
for neglecting the love
to be found
around me daily

EPILOGUE

When you are a thirsty man, even a thimble full of water is welcome. As humans we often forget, simply ignore, or are just blind to the millions of thirsty dreamers that walk amongst us daily.

If we search honestly within ourselves we discover how very thirsty we all really are, thirsty for love, understanding, acceptance and simple kindness.

I was a man crossing the barren desert with a thirst like sand, only to have another soul offer me a caring thimble of water. For this parched traveler it was enough to keep me alive.

If you have found anything within my rambling words, my prayer for you is that it's at least two thimbles full of water to keep the dreamer within you alive.

Peace

Tim 2 Taylor

About the author

Tim 2 Taylor, was a child of the 60's growing up in the slow paced, redneck turbulent south on the outskirts of Atlanta, Georgia. He struggled through the school years as he suffered with undiagnosed dyslexia. A teenage girlfriend gave him his first book of poetry *"The Prophet"* by Kahlil Gibran, which awakened a passion for writing. After graduating, he married his junior high school sweetheart and moved to Florida. Sadly, the marriage ended two years later.

As an adult, Taylor remarried and started a career in advertising. He worked at several nationally ranked agencies as an art director and creative director. Taylor opened his own successful agency 23 years ago -Taylor Productions Inc. He recently launched his second company - Fat As My Dad, LLC.

At the age of 45, Taylor flat lined in the back of an ambulance. Having a near death experience only to be revived, he got a second chance at life. Hence the "2" in his name representing the "2nd " life he's living now.

Within a year he lost 99 pounds and was selected USA Today's 2007 Weight-loss champion and reshaped his life forever.

Currently Tim 2 is a nationally recognized motivational health and fitness speaker, featured in magazines, radio and TV shows. He is the author of the weight loss book "Fat As My Dad."

In recent years Tim 2 has rediscovered his passion for writing poetry. He's excited to present his premiere works "The Found Poet - summer and The Found Poet - winter.

Taylor is happily married and is a dedicated father to his beautiful daughter.

www.thefoundpoet.com • #tim2taylor

Please write a review

If you enjoyed this book please be sure to write a five star review at Amazon.com. In today's book selling marketplace reviews are so important. I really love hearing what people think about my work and by writing a review you can let your voice be heard.

Thanks in advance!

www.ingramcontent.com/pod-product-compliance
Lightning Source LLC
Chambersburg PA
CBHW030509100426
42813CB00002B/404